Rodriguez

Champion Baseball Star

Ken Rappoport

Enslow Publishe
40 Industrial Road
Box 398
Berkeley Heights, NJ 07922
USA

http://www.enslo

Original edition published as *Super Sports Star Alex Rodriguez* in 2004.

Library of Congress Cataloging-in-Publication Data

Rappoport, Ken.
  Alex Rodriguez : champion baseball star / Ken Rappoport.
    p. cm. — (Sports star champions)
  Includes index.
  Summary: "Discusses the life of pro baseball player Alex Rodriguez, including his childhood and early baseball career, his rise to stardom on the Seattle Mariners, his lucrative contracts, and his All-Star career with the New York Yankees"
—Provided by publisher.
  ISBN 978-0-7660-4026-7
  1. Rodriguez, Alex, 1975—Juvenile literature. 2. Baseball players—United States—Biography—Juvenile literature.
I. Title.
  GV865.R62R35 2013
  796.357092—dc23
  [B]

                            2011043754

Future editions:
Paperback ISBN 978-1-4644-0158-9
ePUB ISBN 978-1-4645-1065-6
PDF ISBN 978-1-4646-1065-3

Printed in the United States of America

032012 Lake Book Manufacturing, Inc., Melrose Park, IL

10 9 8 7 6 5 4 3 2 1

To Our Readers: We have done our best to make sure all Internet addresses in this book were active and appropriate when we went to press. However, the author and the publisher have no control over and assume no liability for the material available on those Internet sites or on other Web sites they may link to. Any comments or suggestions can be sent by e-mail to comments@enslow.com or to the address on the back cover.

♻ Enslow Publishers, Inc., is committed to printing our books on recycled paper. The paper in every book contains 10% to 30% post-consumer waste (PCW). The cover board on the outside of each book contains 100% PCW. Our goal is to do our part to help young people and the environment too!

Contents

Introduction

No player in baseball attracts attention like Alex Rodriguez.

It's not only because of his talent but also the high salary he makes. In 2001, after leaving the Seattle Mariners, he signed a record ten-year $252 million contract with the Texas Rangers.

After joining the New York Yankees in 2004, Rodriguez eventually tore up his old contract and signed a new one—a $275 million deal! Naturally, fans expected more from Rodriguez than any other player.

He did not disappoint. He became the only player in major-league history to hit at least 30 home runs and drive in 100 runs for thirteen straight seasons.

Alex Rodriguez is the only major-league player to hit 30 home runs and drive in 100 runs in thirteen consecutive seasons.

Rodriguez is big and strong, one of baseball's best all-around players. Starting out as a shortstop, Rodriguez moved over to third base for the Yankees to accommodate New York shortstop Derek Jeter. Along with his great hitting, Rodriguez is one of the best defensive players in the game. He covers a lot of ground with his long legs and has a powerful arm.

He is one of baseball's nicest stars. He finds time to sign autographs. He likes to talk to fans. Rodriguez is thankful he can be paid so much money to play the game he has loved since he was a kid.

He worked very hard to become a star, reaching the top as fast as he could run around the bases.

Alex Rodriguez began his professional career playing shortstop. But when he was traded to the New York Yankees, Rodriguez had to play a new position at third base.

Alex Rodriguez smashes the ball for a double during Game 5 of the 2009 World Series.

Alex the Great

What was wrong with Alex Rodriguez?

It was the 2009 World Series. The New York Yankees third baseman was struggling. Eight at bats, eight outs in the first two games with the Philadelphia Phillies.

Rodriguez brushed off the mini-slump.

"It's eight at-bats," he told reporters. "I'm not concerned at all."

Not only was Rodriguez 0 for 8, but he had looked weak at the plate. He had managed to hit a ball out of the infield only once in the first two games, striking out six times.

Rodriguez had nothing to apologize for in the 2009 play-offs. He had practically single-handedly carried the Yankees

Alex Rodriguez hits a game-tying two-run home run in the bottom of the ninth inning against the Minnesota Twins during the American League Division Series on October 9, 2009. Rodriguez had been dominant at the plate through the first two rounds of the 2009 playoffs.

on his shoulders with series victories over the Minnesota Twins and the Los Angeles Angels of Anaheim. Rodriguez was awesome: 14 hits, .438 batting average, 5 home runs, 12 RBIs, and 10 runs scored.

However, now in the World Series, it seemed he had completely reverted to form. Despite record hitting achievements through the years during the regular season, Rodriguez had not performed especially well in the postseason.

Rodriguez had gone hitless in eighteen playoff at bats with runners in scoring position dating back to the American League Championship Series in 2004.

But no one on the Yankees seemed concerned with Rodriguez's hitting problems.

"I don't need to tell Alex anything," teammate Johnny Damon said. "He's one of the greatest players of all time. He'll know what to do."

True. Rodriguez was one of baseball's most reliable hitters. During seasons with the Seattle Mariners, Texas Rangers, and Yankees, he did not disappoint. Over his first eighteen years in the major leagues, Rodriguez averaged 42 home runs and 128 RBIs along with a solid .302 batting average.

Alex Rodriguez celebrates with the World Series trophy after winning the clinching game at Yankee Stadium on November 4, 2009.

His performances had earned A-Rod three Most Valuable Player awards. Only one thing was missing: a World Series ring. It was something he wanted most of all.

Rodriguez usually heard boos from Yankee fans for his playoff performances. He quieted them with his red-hot hitting in the first two rounds of the 2009 playoffs.

Then came the World Series, Rodriguez's first.

"I couldn't be more excited," Rodriguez told reporters. "I feel like a 10-year-old kid."

Despite his failure to hit in the first two games of the Series, the Yankees managed a split with the Phillies, who were trying to repeat as world champions.

Game 3 in Philadelphia: Facing Phillies ace Cole Hamels with the Yankees trailing, 3–0, Rodriguez hit a home run. He sparked the Yankees to victory. After his 0-for-8 start, Rodriguez had suddenly regained his home run swing.

In Game 4, Rodriguez came to bat against Phillies ace reliever Brad Lidge with two outs in the ninth inning. Once more, the Yankees' star delivered big time. He knocked in the go-ahead run as the Yankees moved within one game of winning the World Series.

Swinging a red-hot bat, Alex slugged 2 hits and drove in 3 runs in Game 5. He was doing it all for New York—although the Yankees lost that game, 8–6.

The Series returned to New York for Game 6, the Yankees still needing just one victory to clinch.

No home runs this time for Rodriguez, although he was still an offensive factor: One hit in 2 at bats, 2 walks and 2 runs scored as the Yankees beat the Phillies, 7–3, for their twenty-seventh world championship.

And Rodriguez had led the way. In all, he came through with 5 hits and knocked in 6 runs in the final four games of the Series. Rodriguez had finally won his long-cherished championship ring.

CHAPTER TWO

The Next Cal Ripken

Alexander Emmanuel Rodriguez had come a long way. He was born in New York City on July 27, 1975. He grew up around baseball in the Dominican Republic and Miami, Florida. Alex's father, Victor, had played pro baseball, and he taught Alex to love the game. Alex's brother, Joe, taught him something just as important. "He pitched to me in our games and he'd always let me win—until the end of the game," Rodriguez said. "Then he'd go on and beat me. It made me want to get better."

Alex also has a sister, Susy. She helped him with his schoolwork. Their father left the family when Alex was ten. His mother, Lourdes, worked hard to support the family.

As a kid, Alex's older brother, Joe, would pitch to him for practice. Although Joe would beat Alex every time, it helped Alex improve his game. In this photo, Rodriguez takes batting practice for the Yankees.

"It was hard," Rodriguez said. "I did my best to help out around the house and bring home good grades to make my mom proud."

Sports came naturally. He played baseball, football, and basketball. But Alex was not always a star. In his first year on the high school baseball team, Alex had a tough time. His coach told Alex he needed to get stronger. He lifted weights. Every day, he did one hundred push-ups and one hundred sit-ups. Soon, he was one of the best high school players in America. Major-league teams suddenly showed interest.

Every year, major-league teams pick players from high school and college during the draft. Many thought Alex would be the first player selected. He played for Miami

UP CLOSE!

Along with baseball, Alex Rodriguez also starred as a football player in high school. As quarterback for the Miami Westminster Christian High School team, he helped to set a school record for touchdowns.

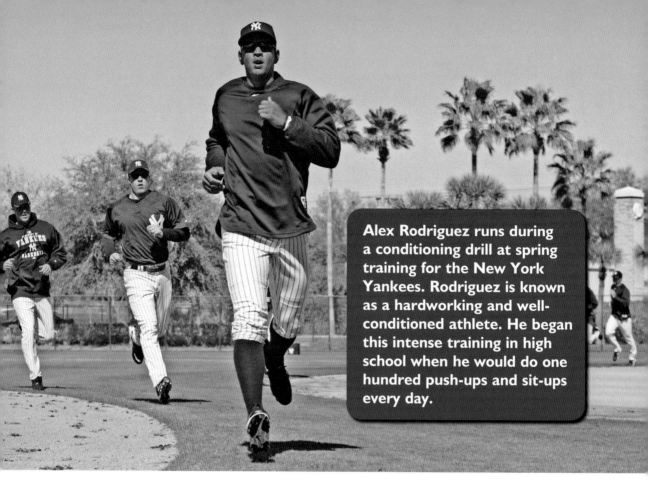

Alex Rodriguez runs during a conditioning drill at spring training for the New York Yankees. Rodriguez is known as a hardworking and well-conditioned athlete. He began this intense training in high school when he would do one hundred push-ups and sit-ups every day.

Westminster Christian High School. He was the national high school player of the year. Alex had led his team to the national championship.

He was called another Cal Ripken, Jr. That was just fine with Alex. The great Baltimore Orioles shortstop was his hero. Like Ripken, Alex was tall, quick, and graceful. He covered a lot of ground at shortstop. He had a good glove, a strong arm, and he could hit with power.

Alex Rodriguez looked up to Cal Ripken, Jr., as a Little League baseball player. Alex even mimicked the way Ripken played shortstop. In this photo, Rodriguez jumps to throw to first base while playing shortstop for the Texas Rangers.

With his family and friends cheering in the background, Alex Rodriguez listens on the telephone as the Seattle Mariners tell him that he has been selected with the first pick in the major-league baseball draft.

Ever since Little League, Alex tried to play just like Ripken. He copied the way Ripken played shortstop, and he imitated the way Ripken hit. He kept the player's poster over his bed. One day, Alex actually met his hero. They were introduced during spring training. Alex was already a high school star. Ripken was impressed. "My first impression was that he was physically mature," Ripken said. "I assumed he'd be a little meek and underdeveloped."

After Alex completed his senior season, there was more excitement to come. On June 3, 1993, he waited for a phone call. Alex was not alone. A group of friends, family, and reporters was at his home in Miami, Florida. They were all waiting. Which team would select Rodriguez in the 1993 baseball draft?

Finally, the phone rang. It was the Seattle Mariners. They had made Alex the top pick! At the age of seventeen, Alex Rodriguez was on his way to the pros.

CHAPTER THREE

Money Player

Everyone was watching Alex Rodriguez.
He had received a $1.36 million signing bonus from the
Seattle Mariners. It was more money than teams usually
give players just out of high school. Could Rodriguez handle
the pressure?

"The main thing they are looking at is how I play,"
Rodriguez said. "Do I play hard? Do I play like I have
money? I don't care how much money I have. I'm working
hard. I'm not saving myself for tomorrow, that's for sure."

Rodriguez started his pro career with a bang. In his first
week, he slammed a 440-foot home run. He was playing

Alex Rodriguez signs autographs at the Kingdome in Seattle, Washington, on September 2, 1993. Reporters and fans wanted a chance to talk and take pictures with the Mariners' teenage shortstop.

for the Appleton Foxes of the Class A Midwest League in the minor leagues. Rodriguez quickly became one of the league's top players.

Everywhere Rodriguez went, people wanted to talk to him and take his picture. Reporters wanted to talk to baseball's new wonder boy. Rodriguez was on the fast track to the major leagues.

Rodriguez moved up to Jacksonville (Florida) in a Class AA league. In his very first at bat there, he hit a home run.

Then he went to Calgary (Canada). Rodriguez was now playing in Triple-A. It was the highest level of minor-league ball. There, Rodriguez ran into problems. He called home. "I was hitting about .200 and I said, 'Mom, I'm tired. I want to come home.' She said, 'I don't want you home with that attitude. Whether you have a month left or three months, you go out and play hard.'"

In the final week of the season, Calgary was tied, 3–3, with Tacoma in the tenth inning. Rodriguez stepped to the plate with a man on base. He took a huge cut and connected. The ball rose higher and higher. Home run! Calgary won, 5–3. Rodriguez had found his stroke again.

By the time his first pro season was over, he had played in all three levels of minor-league ball. The Mariners

Playing for the Seattle Mariners' Triple-A team in Calgary, Alex Rodriguez struggled and was homesick. But his mother told him to keep a positive attitude and play hard. In this photo, A-Rod chases down a foul ball during a minor-league game for the New York Yankees' Triple-A team in Moosic, Pennsylvania, where he was recovering from an injury.

Alex Rodriguez leaps to make a throw after forcing out the runner at second base during a game against the Detroit Tigers on July 26, 1994. The Seattle Mariners gave the young shortstop his first taste of the major leagues in the 1994 season.

brought him up in 1994 to get a taste of the big leagues. He was only eighteen years old. In all, he played 125 games for four teams over five months. He had visited sixteen states and Canada. Not even a broken nose could keep him out of action. "That's a tough road," he said. "I've learned a lot about professional baseball along the way."

Rodriguez was tired. He could have used a vacation. Instead, he headed south to play winter ball. There, he would get more practice. He would also learn more about himself.

A Career Year

Alex Rodriguez was excited. He tightened his seat belt as the plane dipped its wings. The airfield was straight ahead. Out of the window, he could see the island glistening in the sun. He felt he was going home.

The Dominican Republic is a small island nation in the Caribbean Sea. It is a few hundred miles off the United States coast. Its hot weather makes it excellent for playing baseball all year.

Rodriguez had two reasons for going there. He was going to play in one of the top winter leagues. He also would be going back to his family roots. His parents were born in the Dominican Republic, and he had lived there as a young boy.

After the 1994 season ended, Alex Rodriguez traveled to the Dominican Republic to play winter ball and to see the country he had lived in as a young boy. In 2009, Rodriguez wore the uniform of the Dominican Republic in the World Baseball Classic.

"Coming here meant more than working on hitting a curve or the backhand play in the hole," Rodriguez said. "I came to find out where I'm from."

Rodriguez played for a team called Escogido Leones. It was a real test. He faced top pro pitchers. He had a hard time hitting. Alex's batting average was low. He only hit about .200, but he impressed everyone with his superior fielding at shortstop and his great attitude. Rodriguez's manager and coaches liked how hard he worked. So did the fans. He became one of the most popular players in the league. "All I wanted here was not to embarrass myself," Rodriguez said.

In 1995, he played in forty-eight games for the Mariners. He also played in the minors. In 1996, Rodriguez was in spring training. He walked up to Mariners manager Lou Piniella. "I'm ready," Rodriguez said.

"I know you are, son," the Mariners manager answered.

UP CLOSE!

Alex Rodriguez speaks two languages, English and Spanish. He was born in New York City and grew up in Miami, Florida, after a short time in the Dominican Republic.

In 1996, Seattle Mariners manager Lou Piniella named Alex Rodriguez his starting shortstop for opening day. Rodriguez had only played in sixty-five major-league games, but he believed he was ready for the job.

He named Rodriguez as his starting shortstop. Rodriguez was only twenty years old. He had played in only sixty-five major-league games. He was one of the youngest ever to start at shortstop in the majors. And by midseason, he was among the American League batting leaders. He was also on the All-Star team. He was on the cover of *Sports Illustrated*. He was called "The Game's Next Superstar."

Rodriguez finished with a .358 batting average. It was the highest average in the majors. It was also the highest for a right-handed batter since Joe DiMaggio in 1939. Rodriguez's power numbers were amazing for a shortstop. He hit 36 home runs. He set five hitting records for shortstops. He knocked in 123 runs and scored 141. He only made 15 errors. He was named the Sporting News Player of the Year. He also finished second in the Most Valuable Player voting—all this in his first full season in the majors.

It was a sign of great things to come: 42 homers in 1998, 42 in 1999, and 41 in 2000. The power numbers were way over the top for a shortstop, a position that is more highly regarded for its defense than offense.

Rodriguez's contract would soon be running out for the Mariners. When it did, Rodriguez was ready for a change of scenery. Also a windfall of money: $252 million, in fact.

In his first full season in the major leagues, Alex Rodriguez set five hitting records for shortstops. His incredible season was just a glimpse of great things to come.

Alex Rodriguez signed the highest-paying contract in baseball history with the Texas Rangers.

CHAPTER
FIVE

The $252 Million Man

They called him the "$252 Million Man."
That was the amazing contract that Alex Rodriguez signed
with the Texas Rangers.

The contract was the talk of the sports world. Now
Rodriguez had to live up to it. "This is going to be a very
challenging year," he said at the start of the 2001 season.

After his first ten games with the Rangers, he was still
looking for his first home run. Struggling at the plate, he had
only knocked in two runs.

Finally, Rodriguez came to life in a three-game series
against the Oakland Athletics. He blasted 4 home runs and

In his first season with the Texas Rangers, Alex Rodriguez set the single-season record for home runs by a shortstop.

knocked in 13 runs. The Rangers swept the series. Rodriguez was named the American League's Player of the Week.

Rodriguez had again found his home-run swing. In the final weeks of the season, he had an important record within his reach. In 1958, Ernie Banks had hit 47 home runs. It was the major-league record for home runs in a season by a shortstop.

The Rangers were already out of the pennant race. All eyes were now on Rodriguez's race for the home-run record. His team led Anaheim, 5–2, when he stepped to the plate in the fifth inning. The pitcher fired and Rodriguez swung. The crowd started to roar as the ball sailed toward the right-field seats. Home run! Rodriguez had tied the record with

UP CLOSE!

When Alex Rodriguez hit 57 home runs in 2002, he joined Ernie Banks as the only shortstops in major-league history with four straight seasons of 40 or more homers. Banks set the standard from 1957–1960 with the Chicago Cubs.

number 47. Two days later, he hit number 48 to break the record. Rodriguez finished the season with 52 homers.

That would be hard to top. But leave it to Rodriguez to top himself. In 2002, he hit 57 home runs. He knocked in 142 runs. Both were career highs. He was selected the American League's Player of the Year. That was important to Rodriguez. His fellow players had picked him.

In 2003, Rodriguez was again among the top home-run hitters in baseball. He won the American League Most Valuable Player Award. One team general manager called him "the best shortstop ever."

Rodriguez's contract had put him in a special class. He was under great pressure to live up to it. And he did! Playing for a new team, a new manager, and with new teammates, Rodriguez started his time in Texas with two of the greatest seasons in baseball history.

But Rodriguez was unhappy in Texas, even though he continued to have All-Star seasons there. The team was going nowhere. Rodriguez wanted to win a World Series ring. With Rodriguez's encouragement, the Rangers traded him to the New York Yankees in 2004.

Rodriguez had been a shortstop for his entire career. Now the Yankees asked him to learn a new position because

Derek Jeter was the established shortstop with the Yankees. Rodriguez graciously moved over to third base and soon became one of the top defensive players at that position.

Rodriguez continued to pile up MVP awards and All-Star selections. Still, missing from his trophy case: a World Series ring. Rodriguez would have gladly traded in any of his personal awards for such a prize.

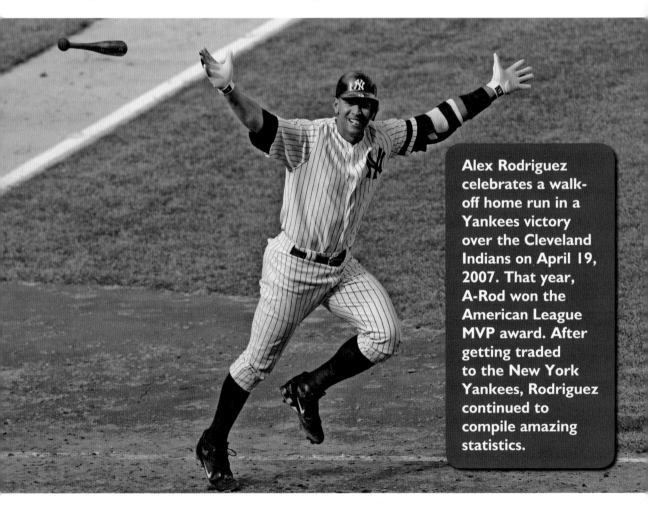

Alex Rodriguez celebrates a walk-off home run in a Yankees victory over the Cleveland Indians on April 19, 2007. That year, A-Rod won the American League MVP award. After getting traded to the New York Yankees, Rodriguez continued to compile amazing statistics.

World Series Hero, and Then Some

It was spring training 2009. As usual, Rodriguez was the center of attention. This time, the news was shocking: He had admitted to using steroids when he played for the Rangers. Other notable players in the game had also used a body-building drug. It resulted in an outbreak of home runs during baseball's infamous "Steroid Era."

"I owe an apology, not only to my teammates, the whole organization, but every fan in the world," Rodriguez said.

A couple of weeks later, Rodriguez had hip surgery, delaying his start to the 2009 season.

Although Alex Rodriguez had a lot of individual success early on with the Yankees, the team did not meet expectations. Much of the blame was placed on A-Rod and his struggles at the plate in the postseason. The steroids scandal brought A-Rod to a low point in his baseball career.

Without Rodriguez in the lineup, the Yankees struggled in the first month of the season with a 13–15 record. On May 8, he returned to the lineup and wasted little time in getting back into the swing of things. On the very first pitch to him, Rodriguez slugged a three-run homer!

One week later, Rodriguez hit a walk-off home run to lead the Yankees past the Minnesota Twins. Then he hit another homer in the ninth inning against Philadelphia to tie the game, which the Yankees won. By early June, the Yankees were in first place thanks to Rodriguez's amazing slugging spree.

But there was more to come. On October 4, 2009, Rodriguez did something very unusual. He hit two home runs in one inning. His 7 RBIs were an American League record for a player in a single inning.

Despite playing in only 124 games that season, Rodriguez still managed to drive in 100 runs and hit 30 homers. It was a record thirteenth straight year that Rodriguez had reached those levels.

In 2009, Rodriguez finally realized his dream of winning a World Series when the Yankees defeated the Philadelphia Phillies in six games. His performance eliminated criticism about his postseason play. For a change, he had played a

Alex Rodriguez watches his two-run home run during Game 3 of the 2009 World Series. The Yankees third baseman had finally achieved his dream of winning a championship.

huge part for the Yankees in both the divisional playoffs and the World Series. His next goal: 600 home runs. Only six other players had accomplished that feat in baseball history.

Rodriguez was closing in on the milestone during the 2010 season. By August, he had slugged 16 home runs to move within one of No. 600. Suddenly, he went into a power slump—no homers in 46 at bats.

Rodriguez knew that number 600 would eventually come, but when? Given the choice, he would have liked to reach the milestone in front of the hometown fans at Yankee Stadium.

On August 4, 2010, he stepped into the batter's box against Toronto's Shaun Marcum with a man on first. Rodriguez had not exactly worn out Marcum with only 4 hits in 17 at bats, including one home run, in his career.

With the count 2–0, Marcum wound up and fired a pitch over the middle of the plate. Rodriguez drove the ball to center field—going, going, gone!

Finally, Rodriguez was in the 600-homer club. He raised his hand in triumph as he rounded the bases and the Yankees crowd roared with delight. All of Rodriguez's teammates came out to greet him after his historic home run.

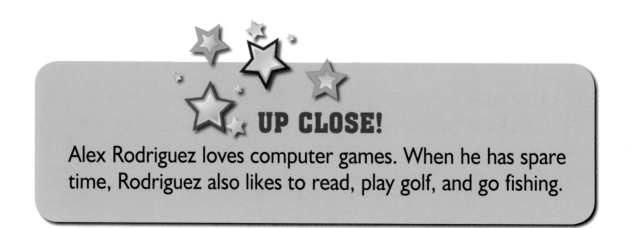

UP CLOSE!

Alex Rodriguez loves computer games. When he has spare time, Rodriguez also likes to read, play golf, and go fishing.

Alex Rodriguez follows through on a grand slam during a game against the Baltimore Orioles on April 23, 2011. A-Rod already became the youngest player to reach 600 career home runs. The Yankees' superstar could break more home-run records before his career is over.

"It sure has been a while," Rodriguez told sportswriters.

Rodriguez became the youngest player in baseball history to reach the 600-homer mark. At thirty-five years, eight days, Rodriguez's home-run pace was far ahead of the rest, including the previous youngest, Babe Ruth.

No telling what other home-run records Rodriguez might set before his career is finished. Without a doubt, Alex Rodriguez has proven he is one of the greatest players in baseball history.

Career Statistics

BATTING REGULAR SEASON CAREER STATS													
YEAR	TEAM	G	AB	R	H	2B	3B	HR	RBI	BB	SO	SB	AVG
1994	SEA	17	54	4	11	0	0	0	2	3	20	3	.204
1995	SEA	48	142	15	33	6	2	5	19	6	42	4	.232
1996	SEA	146	601	141	215	54	1	36	123	59	104	15	.358
1997	SEA	141	587	100	176	40	3	23	84	41	99	29	.300
1998	SEA	161	686	123	213	35	5	42	124	45	121	46	.310
1999	SEA	129	502	110	143	25	0	42	111	56	109	21	.285
2000	SEA	148	554	134	175	34	2	41	132	100	121	15	.316
2001	TEX	162	632	133	201	34	1	52	135	75	131	18	.318
2002	TEX	162	624	125	187	27	2	57	142	87	122	9	.300
2003	TEX	161	607	124	181	30	6	47	118	87	126	17	.298
2004	NYY	155	601	112	172	24	2	36	106	80	131	28	.286
2005	NYY	162	605	124	194	29	1	48	130	91	139	21	.321
2006	NYY	154	572	113	166	26	1	35	121	90	139	15	.290
2007	NYY	158	583	143	183	31	0	54	156	95	120	24	.314
2008	NYY	138	510	104	154	33	0	35	103	65	117	18	.302
2009	NYY	124	444	78	127	17	1	30	100	80	97	14	.286
2010	NYY	137	522	74	141	29	2	30	125	59	98	4	.270
2011	NYY	99	373	67	103	21	0	16	62	47	80	4	.276
CAREER		2,402	9,199	1,824	2,775	495	29	629	1,893	1,166	1,916	305	.302

G–Games played
AB.–At bats
R–Runs

H–Hits
2B–Doubles
3B–Triples

HR.–Home runs
RBI–Runs batted in
BB.–Walks

SO–Strikeouts
SB–Stolen bases
AVG–Batting average

Where to Write to Alex Rodriguez

Mr. Alex Rodriguez
c/o New York Yankees
Yankee Stadium
1 East 161st Street
Bronx, NY 10451

Glossary

All-Star team—The top players are picked each year to play for their league in the All-Star Game. The mid-summer classic matches the American League against the National League.

at bat—A player gets an at bat when he comes to the plate and gets a hit, makes an out, or reaches base on an error. He does not get an at bat if he walks, is hit by a pitch, sacrifices, or hits a sacrifice fly.

draft—A selection of players by major-league teams that take turns choosing the players they want.

major leagues—The American League and National League make up the top professional leagues in baseball.

minor leagues—All the pro leagues below the major leagues. Class A is the lowest level. Class AAA is the highest.

playoffs—Following the end of the regular season, four teams from each of the American and National leagues compete for the World Series championship.

shortstop—The position is part of the "middle infield" with the second baseman. The shortstop usually has the strongest arm of all the infielders.

# Further Reading

Books

Bradley, Michael. *Alex Rodriguez.* New York: Benchmark Books, 2005.

Clark, Travis. *Alex Rodriguez.* Philadelphia: Mason Crest Publishers, 2009.

Smithwick, John. *Meet Alex Rodriguez: Baseball's Lightning Rod.* New York: PowerKids Press, 2007.

Uschan, Michael V. *Alex Rodriguez.* Detroit: Lucent Books, 2011.

Zuehlke, Jeffrey. *Alex Rodriguez.* Minneapolis, Minn.: Lerner Publications, 2009.

Internet Addresses

Baseball-Reference.com: Alex Rodriguez
<http://www.baseball-reference.com/players/r/rodrial01.shtml>

ESPN.com: Alex Rodriguez
<http://espn.go.com/mlb/player/_/id/3115/alex-rodriguez>

The Official Site of The New York Yankees
<http://newyork.yankees.mlb.com/index.jsp?c_id=nyy>

Index